I0528620

Praise for *All Things Holy and Heathen*

"I read Chelsea Jackson's amazing debut collection, *All Things Holy and Heathen*, twice to savor its bodily vitality more deeply. Jackson is shameless and charming, brimming with suffering and healing. They are an inventor of names like 'The One Whose Voice is Lullabies' and 'The One Whose Hands are Stained Red,' and they speak with 'wrung-out lungs screaming for salvation' as they offer us 'the universe's sigil, infinite abundance.' This book is music, is magic, is potent, is precious. Read it and rejoice."
– Alicia Ostriker, author of *Waiting for the Light* and *The Volcano and After: Selected and New Poems, 2002-2020.*

"Visceral, vibrant, magically singular and seductive. Jackson's imagination, style, and refreshing voice lull readers into their haunting world. We are grateful for the invitation into this chaotic realm of memory and reverie and want more and more.
– Jose Hernandez Diaz, author of *The Fire Eater* and *Bad Mexican, Bad American.*

"In *All Things Holy and Heathen*, Jackson sets down a winding path, walking with us as we pluck flowers for their familiar and just-on-the-tip-of-our-tongue aroma, and kick over rocks to inspect the slithering and crawling in the darkness underneath. In the end, it is impossible to come away from the page without feeling as though having peered through a looking glass—reflecting both outwardly, and within—to our future, and throughout our past."
– *Grim and Gilded*

ALL THINGS HOLY & HEATHEN

poems
by Chelsea C. Jackson

APRIL GLOAMING

edited by Lance Ümmenhofer
design by Theo Hall

©2024 by Chelsea C. Jackson

Design ©2024 by Theo Hall

First Edition

All rights reserved. No part of this publication may be reproduced or transmitted in any form or by any means, electronic or mechanical, including photocopy, recording, or any information storage or retrieval system, without permission in writing from the publisher.

Publisher's Cataloguing-in-Publication Data

Jackson, Chelsea C.

All things holy & heathen / written by Chelsea C. Jackson / designed by Theo Hall

ISBN: 978-1-953932-26-6

1. Poetry: General 2. Poetry: American - General I. Title II. Author

Library of Congress Control Number: 2024933702

To Parker, whose love, encouragement, and home-cooked meals made this collection possible.

To the "Jackson Girls," and the blood, tears, and laughter we share.

Contents

The First Human

One quiet day, the Earth's animals decided they needed a project. So, they made humanity. The proud Oak determined she would form the body's trunk. Jealous, Willow added arms and acorn eyes.

Panther skinned a watermelon for the brain and Caterpillar walked labyrinths on its sticky surface, as Whale blow-hole-blew dandelion seeds into synapses. Gorilla used Spider's web to sew in the bones of his deceased brethren, and a bloom of Jellyfish plucked out their tentacles and shapeshifted into organs.

The Bees covered it all in honeycomb, and the Ladybugs scrubbed themselves plain in seafoam, lodged their shells into the ends of the hands and called them fingernails. Hearing the commotion, Seaweed and Moss insisted on joining in and glued themselves haphazardly onto the head and pelvis.

When the creatures had finished, they examined their work and asked, "It is good?"

Life

Every first heartbeat comes
by feeding on the mother
pulling her cells apart
using her up.

Threadbare Flourishing

The wild boar shits and the mushrooms erupt
while a dust-filled wind lifts the branches of the willow
like a boy lifting a sheet to peek at the breasts of his first lover.

This is a gospel of all climax
the never-ending tale of Terra's death
and resurrection. A threadbare flourishing.

The goddess rolling in her own decay
giggling as she sprouts tresses of pine
feeds on pollen, sap, and the corpses of cicadas.

If my body were a house

my eyes would be the door, one look
to determine if you are welcome
onto the porch of my tongue or spit
between teeth like the shell of a sunflower seed.

I would sleep in the dank crook of my knees
but find the best rest in the bed of my fingernails.
My kitchen would be between my legs, thighs
slapping away like pans on the stove.

The bottoms of my feet would be windows
eager to take in soil, sink
into sand, leave a mold. Never dirty.
Always streaked with loam.

I would waltz up my hallway arms
tracing veins as they dare me
to misstep, break
glass shoe on wrist.

I would avoid the closet of my chest.
It's always empty or bursting.

A Tale of Two Wives

I

After the first had flown away, God sat lounging with the newly-named animals. God looked around and told them, "It is not good for man to be alone, but I do not want to be his companion. I will make another."

So God asked the crickets to hum a lullaby, and when Adam was asleep, God called out to Eve, begging her to turn from rib to Helper. And so, Eve came out.

Tearing herself from Adam, she got to work gathering wood, picking almonds, settling fights among the lion cubs, comforting Adam when God stopped answering.

But soon, she grew tired. So she called the crickets, but they would not sing for her. She sat alone wondering when someone would help her, would make her feel less like rib, more like adamah.

II

One day while bathing, Eve noticed two eyes gazing from the bushes of the garden wall. She called out to the eyes, asked if they needed help. Dug a hole under the wall. Crawled among petals, leaves, and worms. Then Eve saw.

Hair knotted like the branches of a fig tree. Sepia skin freckled with constellations leading down to breasts, new and familiar. Navel cavernous and plunging lower to warm life, wild and enfolded. Her eyes were open to all of her, and in seeing, Eve became immersed in her own moist humus.

And no one looked for them for three days.

III

On the third day, Adam called for his second wife and Eve came glowing and breathless. "Why are you covered in dirt?" he scowled. "Go bathe and then pick some carob for our meal. I'm starving."

Clean and broken, Eve ventured to the center of the garden. Picturing her beloved lying beyond the wall, Eve called on Serpent, the most sympathetic of all Eden's creatures. Together they devised a plan.

And so, Eve: Picked fruit. Called for her hungry husband. Sewed him a loincloth. Pretended to be ashamed of her body. Mourned with Serpent as he curled around his lifeless limbs. And tried not to skip as she left Eden.

Squinting through the blaze of Jophiel's sword, she found her love. And as Eve ran to *her*, euphoria seeping from her footsteps, she felt a kick in her womb. A nation of soil rooting inside her.

And the owl screeched.
Lilith wept.
And Adam and his god exhaled in relief.

Pin-Up

inspired by Amy Bennett's painting *Pin-Up*

Bow of flamingo mama, with child's mouth,
door, pock-marked thighs, all ajar
exposed and teetering.

A Quiet Room

prays to the hum of
baby on nipple, shameless
and slurping blessings.

I grew up

in a candy-cane house
with carpets the color of burnt oatmeal
and a Christmas tree growing in the front yard.

Confession: It was not a candy-cane house so much as a red and white trailer.

A moss fortress, its woodstove smoke
straining toward transient glory days passed
grumbling at the deadweight wheels sunken
into swampland and mosquito larvae.

Confession: The Christmas tree in the front yard was the first of my parent's marriage.

The American flag strung up outside and around
our throats, cradling us in lullabies of sacrifice.
Orders and uniforms stuffed behind headboards, buried
under the kitchen's peeling linoleum.

Confession: My father was the smoke. My father was the flag.

The laces of combat boots hung the tree
upside down. Drained it like the deer
dangling in the garage, whose vacant eyes
soon overlooked an empty marriage bed.

Confession: Long since ripped out by new owners, today my mother admits the tree is the only thing from her marriage she wanted to keep.

Black and blue, red and white all over
that family just died. Flatlined.
Another casualty numbers cannot climb to;
no flag big enough to cover the casket.

Confession: Years later, still reeking of smoke and dripping with larvae, I visit the trailer once again.

Remove the bars from the windows
so as not to keep the ghosts hostage.

Carve a grave into the swamp-sponge, whisper
to the moss-encased mausoleum, *sorry for the bloodstains.*

Detach the wheels, my inheritance.
Tuck them in my back pocket.

The young Michelangelo

dissected and sketched cadavers
because you have to start somewhere.

A common Renaissance practice—
artists as anatomical cartographers
charting the tension of tendons
canyons of vertebrae
the beautiful bile of criminals
baptized in the name of science.

Because to know chapels
you must also know the muscle and marrow underneath.

I am a collage

of knickknacks found between couch cushions
and heirlooms stuffed behind closet doors.

Corner-clinging spiderwebs make up my synapses
as candle wax flows from my eyes, hardens on each cheek.

My neck is my grandmother's rainstick;
the clouds follow me wherever I go.

My backbone, the spine of whatever book I'm reading
and family photos turned tattoos

trail down each arm to meet my branch fingers
fashioned from all the splinters I've ever gotten.

My belly button is a cat eye
and dog whiskers spring from my hips.

My legs are tornados.

I draw the moon on my scarred left knee
and the sun on my right.

One foot webbed and drifting in the river,
the other rooting itself on the shore.

Riding the Amtrak to Virginia for the Birth of My Nephew

for Jaxon

I travel the land that raised me to get to you.
Daydream who you will be as I watch the earth change
city to farm, hill-ridden to tidewater-soaked—
the changing leaves and briny air kissing like currents.

No matter the color of your hair (red like your mother
always wanted?) or eyes (green as algae? blue
like the jay in the dogwood?) you, too,
will sprout, flower, wither, and fold into the ground.

Stories soak the soil and drape the sky. So I will teach you
        to open your palms to what the sediment is saying
        to sense change in the weather
        to find the North Star, Venus, and the duo of Dippers
and you can remind me what it is like to exist as stardust and loam.

I will teach you to boogie board—
let you collide with the ruins of the pier.
Its splinters in your skin and my comforts in your ear
you will learn power should not be owned
that life envelops us in wound and wild healing.

I am so excited to meet you, little one.

So excited I had to stop reading to write this poem. So excited
I cannot even be angry at the children in the stained seat next to me
yelling, "Is that the ocean?"—at every stream we pass. But you,

you will know the ocean, my dear,
and the rivers will sway you to sleep.
The sand will stick to you like freckles
and the marsh grasses will offer themselves up as your hair.

What the Weather Taught Me

I.

Instead of Barbie dolls
and glittery makeup sets,
I had a weather kit
and my body.

Those moments when chills up the spine
met summer sweat trickling down
the nape of my neck; warm waters
crashing into low pressure,
a stirring.

II.

The weather became my traitorous playmate
the kind that thickens the skin,
a barometer for cruelty and strength.

Hurricanes showed me what flashlights
and playing cards are for.
Ice storms made sure I knew
the value of a scalding shower.

Three tornados proved sanctuary
can be found in a camp mess hall.
The heat taught me to melt on cue.
The breeze, safe touch.

III.

My kit long fallen apart,
I check my weather app religiously.
Memorize hourly temperature changes,
jet stream patterns, stale meteorologist jokes.

But I still rely on my body
to tell me what the sky is thinking.

The atmosphere vibrates through my vacant chest
like a car, covered in time and branches, still ignites
at the touch of a new battery. Resurrection.

Training Wheels

wretched off, my father and I head for the graveyard,
its sinuous road. After a few pushes and precarious balancing
on my two-tire-tightrope, I am riding toward the dead—
opaque cheerleaders beckoning me forward.

But they grow impatient with my swiveling slowness
and curl their fingers around my handlebars,
veer me left into the canyon-ditch—
the ground hard and unforgiving with drought.

I untangle myself from bike and spirit
smear the blood pooling on my arm
and find my devious audience dissolved.

My father continues with my lesson
until I can pump the pedals sure-footed
and stay on the straight and narrow.

That night we eat veal that days before belonged to another body,
but dirt still coats my tastebuds and I'm cold
no matter how close I inch toward our woodstove.

Decades later part of me still lies among marble and bones—
a child making angels in the freshly-turned earth,
the dead lullabying me into a mausoleum of weeds and baby's breath.

Death

How strange to know death is coming and be shocked
by its arrival. And you left to weep at *what ifs*,
carve words unsaid into decomposing leaves
strewn atop freshly-disturbed ground.

The Names of Death

"The One Who Comes Suddenly"
"The Thread Cutter"
"The Elder Brother of Birth"
"The Mother of Life"
"The Cruel One"
"The Merciful One"
"The Ambivalent One"
"The One Whose Voice is a Howl"
"The Great Motivator"
"The One Swathed in Shadows"
"The Time Keeper"
"The Weapon"
"The Equalizer"
"The One Whose Voice is Lullabies"
"The Trickster"
"The One Whose Hands Are Stained Red"
"The One Constantly Stalking"
"The Pouncing One"
"The One Who Laughs on the Battlefield"
"The Reaper"
"The Saint"
"The Always Hungry"
"The Overworked One"
"The One Who Delivers All to Judgement"
"The Old Friend"
"The Heart Paralyzer"
"The One Who Weeps on the Battlefield"

Dust

I killed a mosquito while receiving Wednesday's ashes.

With the cross on my forehead,
the priest asked me:

When is God most embarrassed by humanity?
When we bleed,
or when we crave blood?

Skirmish Line

You face a sea of deconstructed cardboard boxes—
people demanding breath. And when the sun
glares off your shield, you do not turn away
but stare, blinding yourself.

Until all that exists is the pulse ricocheting
through your ears. Until
screams. Until silence. Until

the sun moves behind a cloud,
your blood frothing, pulled
from a burner like boiling water.
Eyesight still out of focus, you see bodies
strewn about, plucked petals
commanding *forget me not*.
Each with a raised fist mirroring your own
except for the baton you grip tight.

As I imagine Cain looked,
gaze shifting from the rock in his hand
to his brother's head and back again. Cursed,
convincing himself he did what he had to do.

Sweet Inheritance

We eat our stories sugared, then we die. Our bodies leak into soil and sponge-roots; our candied tales evaporate to become the shapeshifting clouds that release the raindrops now breeding in the creek where my children swim, minnows nipping at the skin of their fructose feet. Tonight, I will not taste the laced syrup on my tongue as we turn through family albums and history books.

I Spy

"We should turn the whole Middle East to glass." – Facebook comment
regarding the Iraq War

I spy with my little eye...

*His daughters peer into their glass coffee table
playing their favorite game.*

green polka dots.
Oh, I know! It's the present on the table at the birthday party!
I spy with my little eye...

*The table has been there
as long as they can remember
like a chaotic dollhouse made just for them.
He won't tell them where he got it.*

something gray.
That's easy, the hair on the woman's head, you pick her all the time.
I like her. I think she is wise.
I think she's yucky, kissing that old man like that.

*She's not anything, not any
more than a ghost.*

I spy with my little eye, something black
like our marshmallows after we make s'mores.
Is it this fire pit?
This fire pit?
This fire pit?

*One day they will call them what they are,
will they still want to play games then?*

25

Yeah, the one with the ambulance beside it
and the medicine bottles everywhere.
            I spy with my little eye, something blue.
The sky?
The water in the fountain?
            That water isn't blue, it's red.
It's not red, it's purple.

This lady's dress?
This lady's headscarf?
The rug she kneels on?
            Yep!

        They always look like they're asleep.

                    He doesn't sleep.
                    His children's night-light bounces
                    off the teeth of the embalmed child
                    standing in front of his birthday cake
                    the six candles always aflame.

Ode to White Noise

"Sometimes quiet is violent" – "Car Radio," twenty øne piløts

White noise, I am sorry. I did not feel the kiss of your static on my lobes. Focused
too much on the squawks and ditties in the next room, its great beyond.

I thought it was silence I craved, but it is you. Your blurred edges
seeping into my eardrums like a wave filling the holes dug by crabs at low tide.

I am sorry. I overlooked you. Didn't hear you. Didn't feel your calculated current
electrify my veins. My body. Didn't remember I had a body, fingers, hair, armpits.

I am sorry. Even now this poem isn't about you, but me
rediscovering how to hear. Remembering how shapes taste.

Triangles sharp like cheddar. Circles dripping
like sauce from meatballs. Rectangles a slice of cake

in a bakery display window. It is about me recoiling from the shrill quietude
that comes when the microwave burrito is done;

the clothes are dry;
the fan blades still.

When even our own utterances are swallowed.
White noise in a black hole. Silent. Gone.

Boy in the Museum's Taxidermy Exhibit

"...Between 1914 and 1927, students who were blind or had diminished eyesight partook of special instruction at New York's American Museum of Natural History." – "Blind Kids' Experiences at the Early–20th-Century Museum of Natural History, in Photos," *Slate*, 2014

He starts at the unnaturally dry nose
and feels his way up the head,

its whiskers carving goosebumps into his arms.
Considers spooning out its pupils with his pencil eraser

squeezing so tight their images ooze like the juice
of a grape, flood the lines of his palms. Rivers

to carry him out of his body with its scrawny arms, neck strangled
by his father's old tie. Rivers to glide him downstream

into a jungle with air so heavy-humid
each movement is a knife, slow

and steady through honeycomb. Where the sky
carries birds filled with sickly sweet seeds and song.

Where cat eyes blink above moist nostrils,
and snakes are stuffed with mice instead of cotton.

He feels the chill of their bodies in the coil of his teacher's fingers
around his wrists and snaps out of his sap-coated dreams

as she guides his hands down the empty beast,
plunging him into the solitude of its cavernous chest.

He leaves the eyes and takes the leopard's fang instead.
Makes a blade better than any trinket at the bottom

of a Cracker Jack box, uses it to trim the beast's fur
and fashion a beard for himself. Carries his new toy everywhere.

And his father listens to a radio interview
with Carl Akeley, his mother applies carmine

to her lips, and the Sunday preacher
tells him he has dominion over the earth.

Driving Through the Panhandle of Texas

In these ghost towns, age stains the bloated floorboards
and front porch swings sanded down to their bones
by dust storms and tumbleweed brushstrokes.

As if the land wants to be left alone
as it scratches itself backward through time.

Bloody Tissue on a Subway Station Stair

How did you come to grace
this stage? How many people
witnessed the spectacle?
Your role in the show?

Was the red inkblot soaking your fibers—
spreading to pink around the edges—
a signal of defeat?
A brawl gone too far
in a crowded subway
car? Your entrance an offhanded pass
with eyes cast down and fingers
that dare not touch?

Or was it sickness, cancer, cough? A pulse
craving liberation from the body's closing walls?
A red river's jailbreak turned suicide mission,
drops running against windpipe, chasing
single points of distant light?

Was it a nosebleed, cut, silly mistake?
Was it picking skin raw
to give the heart rest?

Bloody tissue on a subway station stair
from whose pocket, purse, sleeve,
hand did you emerge?

Were you a gift from a man, unhoused
with little more than a cup of copper?
Taken from a bathroom?
Purchased from a local gas-station grocery store—
dual purpose, full service? Bloody tissue

on a subway station stair
stay away from me. You terrify
with your compassion,
your truths.

Controlling the Wind

I was six when I started controlling the wind.
In my sun-spotted yard, I convinced God
to make me a magical Moses.

I would raise my hands and a breeze
would greet my cheeks. Shoots of grass
apples and their leaves shuddered at my power.

I was seven when my cousin drowned.
Determined to retrieve her favorite toy, she jumped
from dock to boat. Found water instead of air.

I was eight when my friend and I broke her hammock,
were left bruised and gasping on the forest floor. Two Tarzans swinging
on a ticking time bomb, taunting its tired strings.

I was ten when my family fractured. Sobbing in my room,
I begged my tears to keep my parents' marriage afloat,
certain I was the storm that sank them.

When I was six, I controlled the wind
and used any magic I had to rustle leaves.

Little Moons

My baby teeth are scattered outside my mother's bathroom window, mixed with the ashes of cigarettes she doesn't think we smell. Nothing will grow in this calcium graveyard, but when it rains, the teeth hover just off the ground, each drop on enamel a tone until they are chattering together, singing the song of the old woman who visited my toddler crib. Little moons singing till they gleam.

Gleaming little moons speckle the ground, giggling as the five-year-old me giggled with the man trapped in the mirror. Little moons gleaming, giggling until ash from the open window sprinkles them sour again.

Soured little moons want to chant themselves into the sky, pull tides, make silly faces at mountains. Silly, soured, little moons carry lullabies taught by spirits, share grins with the restless stuck, grow gardens with the dust of the tooth fairy we so desperately wished for.

My Body as Painted by Salvador Dali

Dawn

I lay splayed across a pallet   resting against the crook of his elbow
dissected into limbs   organs   primary colors

my ribs repurposed as roots   ears turned mushrooms
growing from each calcified curve   my pupils multiplied and blinking
amongst the leaves of the atrophied tree in the left corner

he traces the hair of my body pelvis to crown   to create
a shifting landscape from bush to desert crabgrass   to tangles of seaweed teeming
with radioactive fish plucking at my stomach   nipping
at my fingers in a glowing lake where

at first glance sails dance triumphant in the wind
but upon inspection   just my lungs draped over smokestacks
weeping airbags swaying in a carbon rain

my labia folding around a coral sun

Dusk

Swollen labia sun burns and blinks and bleeds into the Milky Way

my fingernails are filed into stars
ripping holes into the canvas   scabs
on the universe overlooking my teeth turned

beetles   gnashing into sand and shadow
enamel infantry marching on my vertebra and kneecaps   these pilgrim bones leading
to the hollow temple of my wrists   tied together in sacred shelter

my heart nowhere to be found   tucked
under layers of warm paint made cold earth
buried beneath my root-ribs for ghost ants to circle in prayer   as my

remains are scraped from the pallet   left to mingle with coffee grounds and broken bristles

34

Violation

Planets spin on each sand grain
and drop of mud,

every seed stuck and bursting
under your shoe.

You think you're crushing them,
but they're carrying you.

After the raven

Noah sent the dove,
and the dove found a branch around the corner—rested,
stretched, enjoyed some alone time. Laughed
when God commanded, *Take a branch back to Noah.*
Plunged into the waves to ruffle feathers and rinse hope.

Noah sent the dove a second time,
and the dove found a forest boisterous and bountiful—bathed
in the juices of fruit streaming down its breast. Balked
when God urged, *take a branch back to Noah.*
Found a puddle to scrub its nectar-beak clean,

        accidentally coughed up an olive branch on Noah's shoes.

Noah sent the dove a third time,
and the dove found no water to fold into—flirted
with the exhausted clouds. Froze
when God whispered, *please.*
Spurned such holy ego and flew off the edge of the earth.

And God got high off altar ash
as Noah, the divinely chosen,
breathed hot air onto glaciers
bled oil into oceans
burned holes into the heavens.

Hex

mutts, priestesses roll in the mud
to rinse the scent of hunters
whose sweat encrusts their coats

burrs adorn their fur like jewels and fall away
as the women send the clinging ticks off
with a blessing and transform upright and human

deer guide them to the best berries
rabbits cross into their camp to lay
at their hallowed, loam-caked feet

around flame they shriek, they twist
they laugh on the altar of the forest

    ----

the arrows come at dawn. shafts
carved with scripture. tips dipped in wine.

the priestesses' menstrual blood
mixes with the blood of their throats.

the hunters collect their kill.
the meat of the doe caught in the slaughter
will sour in their mouths.

Infinite

The dog seems infinite to the tick.
  The human seems infinite to the dog.
    The stars seem infinite to the human.

And the star-breathing Goddess feels infinitely alone.

Loneliness

"Kenya had three rare all-white giraffes. Two of them...a female and her seven-month-old were found 'in a skeletal state after being killed by armed poachers.'"
– "Two rare white giraffes killed in Kenya," *National Geographic*, 2019

Her eyes were last to lose their glow
as she stretched her still-growing neck toward me
lifted a hoof she would never grow into.
But I was already gone—
my milk nursing the dirt,
the trees, river, and rhino bones
welcoming me back.

We were blank canvases
invitations to begin anew.
But even if you had heard our pleas
over your rifle's roar, what choice did you have

but to paint us with our own blood,
re-make us in your image?

Migration

"Monarch [butterflies] can travel between 50-100 miles a day; it can take up to two months to complete their journey... [In the spring and summer] each successive generation travels farther north. It will take 3-4 generations to reach the northern United States and Canada." – "Monarch Butterfly Migration and Overwintering," U.S. Forest Service

She makes slow work of it
luring them with sugar water and softness
then pinning their parchment wings
between crimson nails.

In the kitchen, she punches holes in the creases
where their black veins meet. The only movement
her threading and the muted TV's flickering
montage of bombed cities.

She closes one eye and flutters a bright corpse
in front of the rubble, creating a second sun.
How gracious I am, she muses.

Outside she prays into each frozen antenna.
Hangs each body on a single branch. Dulled orange dripping
from her new wind chime like the blood of a fresh kill.
An unnatural weeping.

She wants something
beautiful. Something silent.

And rolls her eyes
as the breeze rings through each royal carcass
mimicking the cries of stolen children.

41

Alive: The City

to Philadelphia

In the summer heat, the friction of feet melts the city's asphalt to sludge. A mammoth wave curls over Broad. Cocoons pigeons and taxis. Engulfs cardboard boxes, condos, and their inhabitants. Folds into itself. Layer upon layer, an onyx monster takes shape. Its subway-rail veins rattle with the cries of men and church bells, the rhymes of children on rusting swing sets, the questions of women, the sinking clink of ice in a glass. Life. Blood. The giant greets the retreating clouds and meager sprouts of green burst from its armpit, a nook for eagles to rest and squirrels to shit. The beast tiptoes toward the harbor empty of fish. No one to play with but the rats, bankers, and waitresses, rolling in its syrupy skin. Sometimes they swim, sometimes they drown.

Ode to My Old Cloth Diaper

turned security blanket.
Great soothsayer, glued beneath my nose
rubbing my four-year-old skin raw.

Oh, secret keeper, hugger, bandage,
rotten egg-shell shaded flag I paraded with pride.
Drunk off the sour scent
spilling from your mold-laced fibers,
I begged them not to wash you.

But their plan was more sinister
than I imagined. With guests gone home
birthday streamers pulled down
and a too-heavy bookbag waiting in the corner,
they tucked me in, cooed *goodnight
big girl*, and walked you to your closet grave
crawling with dust and *baby's first* books.

Years after my upper lip healed
and my back assumed a permanent hunch,
I found a shred of you in the closet
and hated my mother.

Quiz on the Back of My Cereal Box

"Women who drink water contaminated with low levels of the weed-killer *atrazine* may be more likely to have irregular menstrual cycles and low estrogen levels...characteristics known to affect fertility." – "Atrazine in Water Tied to Hormonal Irregularities," *Scientific American*, 2011

If we are what we eat...

Will our grandmothers know us
with our pesticide livers and sweet blood?

Will the stars take us back
as their building blocks?

Does the ground refuse to speak to us,
or have we cut off its tongue
and demand it sing?

Yearly Checkup

I'm pretty sure the table is the island
rolled in from the kitchen,
its metal cold on my back.

They don't put me under, but unzip me
forehead to pelvis and down
the inner seam of each thigh.

Peering in, they sigh and get to work.
They decoupage magazine cutouts onto my brain
make my hands itch

with a green rash and an urge to spend.
Program my legs and voice to wobble
if I wander too far, want too much.

They stretch my stomach
and shrink my heart.
Inject insecticides into my uterus.

Already their faces
evaporate from my memory
as I pencil in my next appointment.

Unnamed

One day, as she sat at her handmade kitchen table enjoying a meal and sipping on rainwater, she heard something calling from the forest, its voice bouncing off the trees. Wondering if it was calling for help, she wandered from her meal into the woods to search for the source. She walked up to the trees and asked, *What's wrong? Do you have enough leaves?* And pulled out her hair and draped her strands over their branches. Then she crouched next to an anthill, asked if it had ever been stepped on. And cut off her feet, her toes still in a careful point. Then she leaned back onto the ground and looked up at the sky. Asked if the clouds were ever lonely. Asked, *Is it enough to have each other? Do the beaks of birds tickle? Do the wings of planes slice like a blade on knuckle?* And offered to sing to them, said she knows a tune or two. Then she turned her head to the right and noticed the vines dancing in the breeze. Asked if they wanted a partner, someone to grab onto. And tied herself up. Then she turned to the left and asked a frog, *Do you have enough trees to hop among? Enough hollows to call home?* And transformed herself into a log. Then she whispered to the earth, *Are you rich enough? Are you hungry? Are you dying?* And split herself open, her trunk bursting as termites chewed through the birthmark on the back of her neck and mushrooms lined her chest cavity. But none of them answered her. Not the trees or the anthill. Not the sky or the vines. Not the frog or the earth. And as the ants carried away her liver and the earthworms sewed her eyelids down, she realized the voice she heard was her own.

Gaia

Eyes Aurora Borealis green, she inspects
her spoiling breasts in the bathroom mirror—
ice caps seeping into the bile of her chest
where nothing but heartbeat survives,
where floating fish pulse.

She spits into the sink, pauses
to watch the foam of her curdled oceans
orbit the rubber sun of the drain.
Infection that will soon make its way back inside her,
for nothing truly leaves, everything mutates.   Somewhere,

which is to say, everywhere,
at this moment, which is to say,
always, she sweeps aside the branches
of her *Euphorbia milii* hair, to trace
the handprints seared into her neck

and reaches between bruised thighs, to lift hands
bathed in blood. Bitter she laughs,
vomits cement onto her reflection,
finger-paints "Pangea."
            As terrified men return to her battered door

to harvest her lungs
paint her forests USD green
suck marrow from her bones
take pliers to her toenails and eyelashes
for good measure.

The Day They Came for Science

Magna Mater,

The day they came for science, I bristled
as men toasted their brilliance with petroleum containers
and hammered all the globes flat.

On a mission to rescue you, I prayed to the beetle
and undulated with the seaweed on the ocean floor
until I conceived a hero child. But Great Mother,
nothing was as it should have been.

Labor began and ended with retching,
emptying the plastic and glass of my stomach into the tub.
That's when I found her hunting for hurricanes,
a bright-eyed savior with my nose.

Sparks skating off my tongue, I asked her to listen
to the soft moans of the glaciers. She asked
for five more minutes to practice her cannon balls.

So I tapped my foot to music made by bottles spilling over
the porcelain rim. Said nothing as she waltzed
with the crude oil currents that tickled her feet.

Panicked as she whittled a snorkel from lead pipe
and whispered green-eyed greetings
to the coal-dense mountains trembling outside her window.

And I wept, as she turned lily pads to cinder blocks
hopscotched from her toxic water birth into a yard
budding with milk and honey and ate the sky.

The day they came for science, they came for our children.
With open arms we gave them, and with open arms they went.

Magna Mater, on that day you did not need rescuing
or shared laments about how quickly our children grow up
and find their own ways to destroy themselves and us.

As if you and I were the same.
As if I, too, am not someone's child.

Reclamation

You cannot plant the same tree twice
nor are any two furs
and their bearers identical.

So do not talk of time as the root of healing.

Instead, sing confessions—
songs of petition and praise.

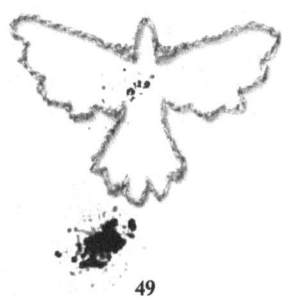

Doomsday Clock

At midnight, the Earth Mother will pare back the bandages
from her fracked fissures and pocked summits
watch mushroom clouds make maps irrelevant
bathe in luminescent dust twirling in the moonlight

as God follows blood streaks on club and stone
and wanders through nuclear shadows
to track down his rabid jewel of creation.
But they will not be found.

For they are writhing in moonbeams
and catching fire in the sun.
Scorched soot swallowed
by that last emancipated rainbow.

Dorsen

"A *Sky News* investigation has found children as young as four working in dangerous Congolese mines where cobalt is extracted for smartphones." – "Meet Dorsen, 8, who mines cobalt to make your smartphone work," *Sky News,* 2017

A boy carrying a mine stumbles
hunched across my screen.

Tells me everything hurts. Tells me
he dreads every morning he wakes up.

No praise on my pillow at sunrise,
he chants to tunes played on shovel.

Hymns no balm for his splintered hands. His chorus keeps tempo
to the steady rhythm of my pointer finger on the "escape" key

as a cotton-sheet-scented candle masks
the smell of death under nails ground to the bed.

Until one day too soon and not soon enough
the boys with the crumbling lungs will take pickaxes to the sky

sift the clouds to find heaven
and race along streets paved with confessions.

Their footprints searing my hands
clasped together in hollow prayer.

Deliverance

Mind of tangled verses and twine,
I swing open my ear and find an end.
Thread the red fibers through my right eye. Pull
to unspool a path, straight and narrow.

I take three steps [in the name of the Father, Son, and Holy Ghost]
before the lifeline turns snare, gives me rope-burn ribs.
My wrung-out lungs screaming for salvation

until I have no choice but to dissolve;
exist only as ash on the split tongue of serpents.
The saints choking on all they burned.

Revival

A mirror allows me to see myself
and see God. And the god in myself
and the part of myself that is in God.

But what to do with a dirty mirror?
The smudged god in it? If my flawed hands
clean it, do I not make it more unclean?
Distorting the image even more? If God can be distorted
by my hand, is he not less of a god?

The rain washes the mirror, the sun dries it,
so I look to them instead. Divinity
in droplets, in the glinting blaze
that refashions them to gemstones.

Self-Portrait as Rain

I am the chime
        vaulting from tin roofs and creek beds
        gravestones and gardens.

I am the drizzle that flirts with the canopy
        bathes the birds
        nurses the catfish and their river.
I am the monsoon that smothers the harvest
        evades the desert.

I am one raindrop too many
        the drop that broke the cloud
        splintered the sky.
The drop that falls on the split lip of the kid
        beat up for wearing nail polish to school.
        I blend with his tears.

I am the deluge that rushes toward storm drains
        carrying needles, fast food cartons, trash.
I am the trash.
I am the poison.
I am the water flushing the wound clean
        rinsing the eye.
I am the eye.
        I do not see myself. I only see myself.
I am the eye and the log in it.
I am the log rotting in the wood
        filled with maggots, decay, and new life.
I am maggots and decay.
I am new life abundant and devoured.
I am devoured. I am disgorged.
I am bile seeping into the ground
        bending through stones and mites to reach the stream.
I am the stream.
I am its brother ocean
        teeming and dying
        welcoming and unrelenting.
I am the wave that reaches the heavens
        the foam that crashes to the sea floor.
I am peace. I am fear.

55

Anxiety Pains

Rocks drop into the slot on my right
shoulder. Pinball against vertebrae and
tendons. I am a receptacle of stones
and shadows, bruised and ajar.

I mutate. Turn my pelvis to a mortar, spine
to pestle, and grind the boulders bulging
through my taut skin. Dislodge the pebbles
clotting vessels like kinks in a hose.
Relieve the heaviness. Replace it with
sediment.

Ivy wraps around each of my scapula,
sewing me into homegrown chain mail.
Flowers use my ribs as picture frames. I am
no longer stone storage but flora, fertilized
by powdered burdens.

Watered by my own marrow. Pollinated
by the bee that slips in from time to time.

My Mother

the cloud, that believed
your rain to be acid.

Feared you would shatter, crash
into the surrounding valleys

drown the saplings, no silver linings left
to stich wounds or braid life vests.

My Cloud Mother, do you see it?
The twinkle in our hazel?

Gaze into the mirror of my grandmother eyes
and find rest. Pour down

and build your house.
Snap the timbers to attention. Twirl

as you plant their seedling brothers. Put aside
the bottle and peek into my chest cavity.

Let out the breath I've been holding
for you. Pluck my ribs, harvest them

for hairpins. Empty my ventricles for nail polish.
Let the generation you tended with tears

grieve and help you reimagine what you lost.
And when we are done, place your back on mine

as we link arms and conspire with the mountains.
Our sweat brimming with sentience.

Igbo Landing

"Igbo Landing is a historic site at Dunbar Creek on St. Simons Island, Glynn County, Georgia. It is the site of one of the largest mass suicides of enslaved people in history." – "The tragic yet resilient story of Igbo slaves who committed mass suicide off U.S. coast in 1803," *Face2face Africa*, 2018

"[The Igbo] rose up in the sky and turned themselves into buzzards and flew right back to Africa…Everybody knows about them." – Wallace Quarterman, 1930

Sunken sanctuary where boats dare not go
fear they'll run aground on robbed flesh, raging ghosts.
Where dignity was claimed in breaths not taken
    the choiceless choices.

While the sea swallowed a pack of murderers
their bodies blending with the curve of the earth,
hallowed mud saw the stolen steal back their heels
    walk to their brine rebirth.

Igbo Landing, where the swamp gave way to skin
dark as the crow. With speckles of seaweed
in their eyes, the Igbo looked up, thought,
    Now that's a good way to go.

The Fall

Then

The stars fell like bullets.
A gentle weeping as billions of crinkled tacks uncoupled from a twilight sky

landing on pillows of rainforest and pools of saltwater,
encircling children turned witches and dragons in the park.

Their *tinks* and *dops* resounding across a heaven that no longer caressed them,
that purged them only to realize it alone was darkness.

Now

Instead of flowers we give bouquets of cosmic bodies.
We carry the celestial marbles in our pockets
and make mandalas for strangers to stumble upon.

We cut up our power bills.
We explore the bottom of the ocean and then leave it alone.

We do not add more work hours with the light.
We do not forge new weapons.

And the Earth glows like a fresh secret
like a flashlight under a heavy quilt.

Great Red Spot

"Jupiter's Great Red Spot is shrinking and could vanish within the next 10 to 20 years." – "Jupiter's Great Red Spot to Disappear in 10 Years?" *National Geographic*, 2018

A lonely iris spins, wedged like a rock between two currents,
once hungry enough to devour the Earth three times over.

I used to believe the stain would always be there—
a thumbprint of the gods, as much a fixture on the universe

as the mole on my neck or scar on my knee.
But the skin wrinkles to dust,

rage evaporates to cloud,
and eventually, all living things stop eating.

And when the bloodshot eye winks its last,
it will share its chaos-forged wisdom,

*Just because something will die
doesn't mean it must be killed.*

Eight

legs on a spider
teeth in each quadrant of the human mouth
months of gestation for a hippopotamus

Eight

planets in this solar system
spokes on the helm of a ship
tentacles on an octopus

Eight

Beatitudes
Angels carrying Allah
Sabbats
Days of candlelight
Practices of the Buddha

The universe's sigil, *infinite abundance.*

The shape a scouting honeybee dances
upon its return to the hive.

Honeysuckle: A Ghazal

A swamp child of the Chesapeake, of the honeysuckle
with sloshing nectar belly, I waded in a bed of creek and honeysuckle.

Each sticky summer night I colluded with the Elephant-Hawk Moth's
protracting proboscis, filling our cheeks with honeysuckle.

Even now, amid the melancholy maturity brings, I catch their scent
before they catch my eye. O sweet reek of the honeysuckle.

My corpse revived by the sickly smell. Drooling,
the child behind my ribcage shrieks, suckles honey.

One flower's candy fluid a pitiful harvest. I pull fistfuls.
Every flower mourns its twin, weeps *goodbye sister honeysuckle*.

Possessed, I march to melody of wind through tubular blossom,
rain on petal, the beat of the invasive honeysuckle.

The gentle tug of calyx, slide of style, surge of stigma
dripping her carnal whisper over this body weak; *honey, suckle*.

Unceasingly, I thank the bush, kneel at her feet.
Draped in white, my priestess the honeysuckle.

Who am I to shower her with praise? Her flesh
turned mutilated feast, the honeysuckle.

It has taken me years to write of this haven,
this tiny joy, to speak of the honeysuckle.

The Hermit's Tutorial: How to Build Your Coffin

I. Gather four wooden boards—
       one from the head of your bed
       one from a footbridge connecting opposing banks
       one from your desk, imprinted
           with love letters and shopping lists
       one from the tallest tree you can find.
    Leave the forest an offering for its gift.

II. Use the bones of your fingers
     to nail the boards together.

III. Take the stones on which you treaded during pilgrimage.
     Lay them down—a mosaic to form the coffin's bottom.

IV. Pour wax from a candle to seal everything together.

V.   Sew a pillow out of your hair. Rest.

VI. No lid is needed. Instead, stargaze
     until centipedes chew holes through your eyes
     and basil grows from your nostrils.

     For you are gone.
     You are garden.

Acknowledgements

I am grateful to the following publications where my work has appeared, sometimes in an earlier form.

Beyond Queer Words – "My Body as Painted by Salvador Dali"

Coffin Bell Journal – "The Hermit's Tutorial: How to Build Your Coffin"

Driftwood Press – "Gaia"

Fatal Flaw Literary Magazine – "Yearly Checkup"

Passengers Journal – "I grew up"

Platform Review – "Infinite"

Riverfeet Press – "Honeysuckle: A Ghazal"

The Write Launch – "Alive: The City" and "Bloody Tissue on a Subway Station Stair"

Tiny Seed Literary Journal – "I Spy"

Touchstone Literary Magazine – "After the raven"

Notes

"A Tale of Two Wives" (pg. 7) – This piece reimagines the Garden of Eden story (found in Genesis 2:4–3:24), specifically the relationship between Adam's "first wife," Lilith—who is said to have flown from Eden after refusing to lie beneath Adam during sex—and Eve, the supposedly docile, curious companion we know today.

Also, *adamah* may be translated as "ground" or "earth" in Biblical Hebrew, hence the use of the name "Adam" in the Genesis creation story.

"Pin-Up" (pg. 9) – This ekphrastic poem was written in response to Amy Bennett's photograph "Pin-Up" found in her *Nuclear Family* exhibit. I toured this and other powerful exhibits at the Brattleboro Museum and Art Center while in Brattleboro, VT, on a DIY writing retreat.

Also, a big shoutout to hosts Liza and Rick, whose church turned stained glass studio turned short-term rental, provided me the perfect place to slow down and work on this manuscript.

"The Names of Death" (pg. 21) – This piece was inspired by an excerpt from *Names of the Lion* written by the 10th-century Arabic scholar Ibn Khalawayh (and translated by David Larsen). I first came across the excerpt in the book *The Technicians of the Sacred: A Range of Poetries from Africa, America, Asia, Europe, and Oceania*, which is a fantastic anthology edited by Jerome Rothenberg.

"Ode to White Noise" (pg. 27) – This ekphrastic piece was written in response to James Johnson and Erin Murray's show *To Let*, which I viewed at the Vox Populi Gallery in Philadelphia in 2019. The epigraph is a line from the twenty øne piløts' 2011 song "Car Radio."

"Boy in the Museum's Taxidermy Exhibit" (pg. 28) – This is an ekphrastic piece inspired by a 1926 photo found in the "General guide to the exhibition halls of the American Museum of Natural History," which captures students in a sight conservation class undergoing the Museum's *Story of Our Furs* lesson. The epigraph is from the *Slate* article "Blind Kids' Experiences at the Early–20th-Century Museum of Natural History, in Photos," by Rebecca Onion and published on December 22, 2014.

67

Carl Ackley was an American taxidermist and biologist around the turn of the 20th century. He is considered the "Father of Modern Taxidermy" and made notable contributions to museums across the United States. Throughout his career, he went on several "expeditions" to Africa, where he killed and collected countless specimens, including a leopard he strangled with his own hands in Somaliland in 1896. Nearly thirty years later, in the 1920s, he started questioning his methods of studying and obtaining wildlife and began working toward animal conservation.

Carmine is a red dye extract used in makeup and food products. It is made by powdering the exoskeleton of the female cochineal beetle.

"After the raven" (pg. 37) – This piece reimagines the biblical story of Noah sending the dove out after the flood (found in Genesis 8:6–12).

"Hex" (pg. 38) – The opening phrase "mutts, priestesses" is borrowed from Patricia Smith's poem "What Was the First Sound" in her powerhouse of a collection *Blood Dazzler*, published in 2008.

"Loneliness" (pg. 40) – The epigraph for this poem is from *National Geographic*'s article, "Two rare white giraffes killed in Kenya," written by Natasha Daly and published on March 11, 2020.

"Migration" (pg. 41) – The epigraph for this piece is taken from the U.S. Forest Service and USDA webpage on "Monarch Butterfly Migration and Overwintering."

"Quiz on the Back of My Cereal Box" (pg. 44) – This epigraph is from *Scientific American*'s article "Atrazine in Water Tied to Hormonal Irregularities," written by Lindsey Konkel and published on November 28, 2011.

"Gaia" (pg. 47) – According to the Encyclopedia Britannica and other sources, the "*Euphorbia milii*, or the "Crown of Thorns" plant, is often referred to as the "Christ Plant" or the "Christ Thorn." Some legends claim this is the plant used for Jesus' crown during his crucifixion.

"Doomsday Clock" (pg. 51) – The Doomsday Clock is a tool and symbol that warns the public of how close humanity is toward a global catastrophe of our own making. It was created in 1947 by atomic scientists trying to educate the public on the dangers of nuclear weapons. In January 2023, the clock was set to 90 seconds before midnight, the closest it has ever been to doomsday.

68

"Dorsen" (pg. 52) – The epigraph for this piece is from the *Sky News* article, "Meet Dorsen, 8, who mines cobalt to make your smartphone work," written by Alex Crawford and published on February 28, 2017.

"Self-Portrait as Rain" (pg. 55) – This piece was inspired by "The Thunder, Perfect Mind," an ancient Gnostic text whose author is unknown.

"Igbo Landing" (pg. 58) – These two epigraphs are from *Face2face Africa's* article, "The tragic yet resilient story of Igbo slaves who committed mass suicide off U.S. coast in 1803," written by Bridget Boakye and published on June 12, 2018. It's important to note that Wallace Quarterman was one of the formerly enslaved individuals interviewed for the Works Progress Administration's Federal Writers Project, which was launched in 1935 and disbanded in 1943. Quarterman was interviewed by Zora Neale Hurston [with Alan Lomax], and those interviews can be heard or read via the Library of Congress' website.

Throughout the writing and honing of this piece, I sought to respect the sacredness of this story and the resilient act it recounts. The realities of slavery and its continued impact are part of U.S. history and remain a painful aspect of Southern inheritance. Knowing stories like Igbo Landing is vital if we are to reckon with our past and co-create a more just future.

To read more about this legend and its many variations, please see the following resources:
- *The Legacy of Ibo Landing: Gullah Roots of African American Culture* by Marquetta L. Goodwine
- *The People Could Fly: American Black Folktales* by Virginia Hamilton
- *Black Folktales* by Julius Lester
- *The Flying Africans: Extent and Strength of the Myth in the Americas* by Lorna McDaniel (essay)

"Great Red Spot" (pg. 60) – The epigraph for this piece is from the *National Geographic* article, "Jupiter's Great Red Spot to Disappear in 10 Years?" written by Nadia Drake and published on February 21, 2018.

"The Hermit's Tutorial: How to Build Your Coffin" (pg. 63) – This ekphrastic poem was inspired by the Hermit card in Fabio Listrani's *Santa Muerte Tarot* deck.

Gratitude

The early rumblings of this collection began during my time in Drew University's MFA program. Deepest gratitude to my mentors, Afaa Michael Weaver, Sarah Vap, Judith Vollmer, and Alicia Ostriker; your wisdom and the time you spent with some of these poems are invaluable. And thank you to Sean Nevin and all my fellow poets and professors at Drew [including those I studied under in the Theological School]. You have each left a fingerprint on my writing; for that, I am grateful.

I'm especially grateful to fellow Drew MFAers Jake, Emmie, Emily, and Chelsea. Thank you for all the workshopping and for attempting 30in30s with me each April. (Why do we do that to ourselves again?) And a huge shoutout to the writers and readers I have worked with, taught, and written alongside these last few years, including Cathleen (your passion for uplifting the next generation of writers is inspiring), Rosanna, AJ, and my fellow team members at *The Maine Review*.

Thank you to my friends and family who support my goals and cheer me on. To Chenay, Mike, Ashlin, Laurel, Robb, Cathy, Lisa, Robert, Hans, Nancy, Cory, Nick, Dad, Molly, LaVonna, and Cliff, you each contributed to this book in your own way, and I am lucky to have each of you in my life.

So much of this book is a spell for our collective liberation. I would not understand that or the responsibility of this word-filled magic without Ash, Christina, Deb, Kelly, and Brenna. Thank you.

And to the artists and ancestors blood-related and beyond who planted seeds of liberation, imagination, and resistance-filled joy, I honor you. May we nurture these inheritances well.

Finally, to my mom, Lisa, and my sisters, Holly and Rilee, thank you for believing in me and my vision even when you couldn't fully understand it. So much of who I am is because of the three of you, and I am so grateful to be a "Jackson Girl."

Lastly, this work would not exist without the love and support of my partner, Parker Loesch, who not only encourages me to pursue writing but also takes on other responsibilities and provides the time, space, and patience for me to do so. Park, you have all my gratitude and love.

And thank you, reader, for offering your time and energy to this collection. I do not take it for granted. My hope is this book left you with something: joy, anger, questions, an idea, a stirring. But no matter how you leave these pages, I hope we continue lifting one another up and co-creating a world where we can all grow—interconnected and flourishing.

Chelsea C. Jackson (they/she) is a cross-genre writer, editor, and literary consultant. They believe creativity is a catalyst for change and use their work to ask hard questions, interrogate inherited social narratives, and explore what it means to be human. Chelsea holds an MDiv and MFA in Poetry from Drew University, is the Co-Editor of *The Maine Review*, and offers workshops, classes, and other events to foster community and support writers in their writing and publishing goals. Chelsea is published in *Riverfeet Press, Fatal Flaw Literary Magazine, Coffin Bell Journal, Bridge Eight, Hearth and Coffin Literary Journal*, and *Beyond Queer Words*, among other publications, and was a finalist in the *2020 Driftwood Press In-House Poetry Contest* and the *2022 Animal Heart Poetry Collection Contest*. After moving around for over a decade, they recently returned to their home state of Virginia to help co-create a more just, equitable, and eco-conscious "New South," be closer to family (and the water), and vie for the title of "Coolest Auntie." They live in Richmond with their partner and cuddly pitbull. You can connect with them at chelsea-jackson.com or on Instagram/X/TikTok @sea_c_j.